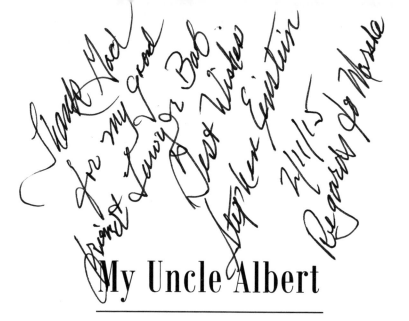

My Uncle Albert

Five years of Discovery

D1621942

STEPHEN I. EINSTEIN

PAGE PUBLISHING, INC.
New York, NY

First originally published by Page Publishing, Inc. 2015

ISBN 978-1-63417-059-8 (pbk)
ISBN 978-1-63417-060-4 (digital)

Printed in the United States of America

Acknowledgments

First and foremost, this book is to honor my sister, Greta, who has since passed on. Without her vision and pure genius, this book would have never come to be.

To my dear old friend and mentor, Sid G., this book would never had been written if it wasn't for you pushing the idea down my throat.

Stephen I. Einstein

Preface

Albert Einstein was one of a kind, and I should know because he was my uncle, and I knew him better than the rest of the world. My name is Stephen Einstein, and I am the last blood relative on this planet.

I lived with my uncle Albert for five summers starting every April to September from 1950 to 1955. After leaving my uncle in September of 1955, he suddenly died of a massive coronary. The loss was great; he was very good and loving to me. The knowledge that was passed on to me over those five years was literally priceless.

Before he died, I got to know the real Einstein. Join me on this exciting journey, so you too can get to know a genius, the very first man crowned Man of the Century, not to mention one of the few people in recorded history to receive the Nobel Peace Prize in 1929.

Truth be known, that is before I was born, my uncle Albert and my father never got along. You will discover that there were multiple reasons for this.

As famous as my uncle was, he never let it go to his head. He was really a very shy, loving man. However, his actions were totally outrageous.

I loved my uncle more than I could possibly say, but I hope there isn't another Albert Einstein out there, and the main reason for this fact is because I don't think that I could take another one like him.

When most tried to understand my uncle, they would constantly be looking high up on the ladder of intelligence, when in reality he was a very simplistic man with his feet planted firmly on the ground.

Living with my uncle from 1950 to 1955 was the greatest experience that I would ever encounter the rest of my life. You will also have proof positive that this little man was a giant among his peers from a very early age.

Albert Einstein was a true visionary with uncanny insight into everyday living. I was shown at a very early age that everything in life is relative to everything else, and people all over the world are pretty much the same. The differences that are present are things like color, where they live, different types of food, and heritage. But beyond all of that, what remains is that we all cry, feel sadness, feel happiness, and so on. We remain all human beings inside.

My uncle was short, but he had more understanding and heart than most people I would ever meet in my lifetime. He would often tell me, for every action there is an equal and opposite reaction. He would tell me time and time again, "Be very careful the decisions you make in life, they may come back to haunt you in the future." Every time he would tell me that, I would laugh. He would look at me in very serious face and say, "You better believe what I'm telling you, or it may be your demise. And furthermore, just remember, animals are smarter than most human beings I have ever met." After he said that to me time and time again, it finally started to sink in, and eventually, I began to believe what he was trying to tell me. Everything is relative to everything else.

So if you will come with me on an amazing journey into the mind of my uncle, the genius, a man who was totally outrageous but very human and down-to-earth, I promise you a story of enlightenment, growth in yourself as a human being, and a journey that is not boring. Come with me on the five years of discovery that for the most part made me the person I am today—Stephen I. Einstein, nephew of one of the greatest men who ever lived, Albert Einstein, first man to ever be named Man of the Century.

Year One of Discoveries

I was born on September 10, 1945. According to my mother, I was a breech birth, and according to my mother, the whole hospital heard my arrival at one twenty in the morning. Unbeknownst to me at the time, I was already very famous. I was to be the very last male Einstein born. But this story is not just about me; it also has to do with a very famous man, a man to be crowned the Man of the Century. He never lived long enough to share in his own glory. The person I'm referring to is my uncle Albert, Albert Einstein to be exact.

We need to return to where it all started—the very beginning. I assure you that there are some people who will be able to relate to events that took place; the majority will find events to be very shocking and distasteful. So let's begin this journey together. As painful as it might be to me, it must be told now that everyone is dead and in no way will I be disrespecting any of my family. This is my story, and unfortunately, I'm sticking to it.

Actually, my nightmare begins the night of my fourth birthday. To this day, I still don't know what caused the terrible fight between my mother and father, but I guess after all this time, it doesn't really matter anymore. My father walked out on my mother that night, and eventually I found out he had gone to Florida for a year. When he did, all credit cards were stopped of my mothers, and all cash accounts were closed. In a heartbeat, my mother and I were poor. She found us a place in Flushing, New York. Thank God my mom always carried a great deal of cash on her, or else we might have been homeless. We had an apartment over a bar, and I guarantee you it was anything but peace and quiet.

Mother finally found a job in New York City, which was about twenty or so miles from where we had the apartment. Her boss, she said, was very much a gentlemen and very high in his organization. She was his personal secretary. He was so nice that she was able to call him by his first name, which was Jesse. One Sunday afternoon, she had invited Jesse over for dinner. When we finished dinner, Jesse and I sat down in the living room. Eventually, my mother joined us, and we just sat around talking and relaxing after that terrific dinner my mom had prepared. What happened next was to change all three of our lives forever. That lovely Sunday afternoon I was kidnapped from my mother's arms by five very big men with even bigger guns. I never saw my mother again for thirteen years. If you think that was bad, read on and you will discover that wasn't the worst of it; the real horror was yet to come. They brought me downstairs and pushed me into one of the three black limos that were waiting. A woman I had never set eyes on before stuck me with a needle in my neck, then everything went black.

It must have been many hours later when I struggled to open my eyes. The first thing I saw was my father staring into my face. He had the biggest smile I had ever seen. It was like he had finished the most delicious candy bar he had ever had and was ready for another. To explain his facial features more clearly, it was like he had acquired another company for next to nothing. My father, amongst other things, was a corporate raider. For those who don't know what that is, I will explain. Like the cutthroat businessman he is, he would overpower the shares in any corporation that was going under and buy the shares for next to nothing to own that company by having the majority of shares on the open market.

"Hello, son, it's been a long time since I've seen you. Now you're back where you belong, with me."

My first sentence to him was, "Dad, you could have done this differently. All you had to do was ask for me to visit. You didn't have to cause all of this drama."

Little did I know that my journey into the bowels of hell was just about to begin, and it was to last thirteen years before I would win my freedom, but that's another story for another time.

Many months had passed, and I didn't keep track of how many, but one night when I was through with my chores of washing toilets, floors, and garbage cans in the restaurant, he asked me to have dinner with him and Joseph, who was his number one bodyguard and chauffer. At dinner he revealed, to his satisfaction and gratification, of course, the plans he had made for me, and it wasn't up for negotiation.

"My son, you are way ahead of your time and very intelligent. You are four years old and have the mind of a twenty-year-old. Whether you know it or not, you have a very famous uncle. He and I have never seen eye to eye. We have just gone our separate ways, but when he and I talk, we are civil to each other, barely. You're going to be very famous some-day, and I want to be the father of that little boy sitting across the table from me.

"Your uncle's name is Albert Einstein, and he is a physicist. He is known worldwide for his many accomplishments. As an example, he was awarded the Nobel Peace Prize in 1929, and that doesn't even scratch the surface of his fame. I want you to spend time with him every year. I've talked with him about this, and he is anxious to meet his nephew. So Monday morning Joseph will be taking you down to Princeton, New Jersey, where he lives. Albert has a house in walking distance of his laboratories at Princeton University. I really think you will like him, Steve, and I expect you to get along with him. Pick his brains for anything and everything. Do you understand what I'm saying?"

"Yes, I understand exactly what you're saying."

"Okay then, this weekend, Irene will help you pack after she takes you shopping for a lot of new clothes. You and Joseph leave at first dawn Monday morning. By the way, son, I want you to try and get along with your new stepmother. She can be a very nice person if you let her. She is my wife now, and I expect you to be on your best behavior when you're with her."

My head literally ached, my mind felt like a whirlpool of thoughts, and many questions were yet to be answered. Whether I liked it or not, Monday was going to be here in three days. But for now, I was going to have a very busy weekend getting ready to jump into the unknown.

When the alarm went off, it was still very black outside except for the huge floodlights that came on at night when everyone went to bed. Sunrise was at the horizon; it would be light very soon. As my eyes opened fully, I was facing the window, and I couldn't help but seeing and hearing the torrential rainfall, and it was also pounding on the roof of the restaurant. I remember saying to myself, "What a disgusting weather day to take a trip. I hope Joseph is a safe driver and has a lot of patience today."

After putting my robe and slippers on, I went out into the kitchen for something to eat. When I walked into the kitchen, my father and Irene were already having coffee and smoking their stinky cancer sticks. I knew every one they smoked was another nail in their coffin. But I never said anything. What do I know— I'm just a kid. It was just another something I had to put up with while I was triying to eat my breakfast. I remember thinking as I sat a few feet away from that terrible smell while I was trying to eat my cereal that I had hoped my uncle Albert didn't smoke, but that wish was very short-lived. After a second large bowl of cereal, Joseph walked in and announced that the big limo was all checked and gassed up. I excused myself and went to get ready for the trip. After a nice hot shower and a new outfit, one of many Irene had bought for me, it was time to join Joseph and say good-bye to my father and Irene. I was excited and very nervous all at the same time. So bring it on, let's have an adventure, one that I'm sure I'd never forget.

Joseph loaded the huge trunk with my suitcases, also bought by Irene, then off we went. My father had the presence of mind to ask Irene to pack some sandwiches and soda in a small Coleman cooler. She, for whatever reason, included some candy bars and potato chips in a big brown bag.

The roads were very wet and very slippery, so Joseph took his time till we reached the superhighways. It was slow going until we reached Albany and entered the New York Thruway. We went through the tollbooth, and Joseph was handed this ticket that had to be handed in at the end of the line with money.

Joseph looked over his shoulder and asked if I was getting hungry. Oh yes, I'm very hungry. Joseph return answer was, "It's approaching noon, so Master Stephen, I'm going to get off at the next rest area so we can use the bathroom and eat." "That's just fine with me Joseph, let's do it because I really have to pee."

After using the bathroom and washing our hands, I then realized just how hungry I really was. I ate everything in sight and my soda. Then I started to polish off some candy bars and finished with some potato chips.

"Master Stephen, do you always eat this much?" Joseph asked with a curious look on his face.

"Well, since you asked Joseph, I usually eat more, but I don't want you to think I was a pig. Anyway I did want to leave some food for you, you must be hungry too."

"Oh, just a little, I have been meaning to lose some weight," replied Joseph with a curious kind of expression on his face. Joseph stood about six feet and his weight must have been around 250 pounds. He looked like a big teddy bear, but I wouldn't advise anyone to threaten the family or piss him off; he was mostly muscle, very developed muscle.

Joseph wore his hair very short and always had a chauffer's hat on. But the bulge on his left side wasn't fat it was a .357 Magnum long barrel in his shoulder holster. That sucker could penetrate anything and no one in their right mind would want to be shot with that cannon. My father had the exact same one, and he would put it on whenever he had to leave the restaurant, whether it was to bring money to the First National Bank or go on a buying trip.

"Master Stephen, it's time we take off and continue on to New Jersey. Time is moving on, and I need to get you to your uncle Albert. He is expecting you for dinner, then I need to make the return trip as soon as possible. Your father always needs something taken care of, and I am his right-hand man. How would you like to ride up front with me? Well then, come up front and buckle your seat belt. We are off to Uncle Albert's house."

Once I was settled up front with Joseph and my seat belt was fastened, off we went. It was a much different feeling to sit up front with Joseph than to be just a passenger in the backseat. I had a panoramic view of the world, and it was fantastic.

All of a sudden I was getting very tired; it was part of my chemistry, I guess. Every time I would have a big meal, my whole body would become very tired and it followed me into adult hood. Without any warning whatsoever, blackness started to envelope me and I was sinking lower and lower. Before it took complete control of me, I heard Joseph's voice off in the distance, saying "Master Steve, we are entering New Jersey. We will be in Princeton in a very few minutes." Then everything went black. Then the next thing I remember was Joseph tugging at my shirt, trying to wake me up. "We are here, Master Steve. We have arrived at your uncle's house, please wake up." Well, that was enough to bring me out of the blackness. As soon as my eyes opened fully, I looked around at this huge house, with the biggest front door I had ever seen. It reminded me of the doors you might see in a scary movie. Joseph stepped out of the car and walked around to the back where the trunk release had already opened the rather large compartment. I unbuckled my seat belt and joined Joseph by the trunk. He removed my luggage and brought every piece to the front door. The door was so much bigger than I was, it was absolutely intimidating.

"Well, Master Steve, you're here. Are you going to stare at the door or ring the bell?"

"Oh, I'm sorry, Joseph, I'm somewhere between nervous and nervous."

"Master Steve, just ring the bell, I'm sure it won't bite you."

As I reached for the bell, the old door with a very loud creaking sound began to open and it instantly reminded me of a movie set that was making a horror movie. When it was fully opened, it revealed a very short man that looked like he had lived on the street for years. His hair went in so many different direction that there was no definite style to it. He had two different colored socks on and it was covered by slippers that he might have gotten in another century or out of somebody's garbage can. The little man was holding a pipe and his eyes drooped down to his cheek bones. Instantly, his demeanor changed and his face lit up like a Christmas tree, with a smile that went from one side of his face to the other. He looked down at me and in his broken English with that distinctive German accent he said, "Welcome, nephew, it is so wonderful to finally meet you after so long. Please come in and make yourself comfortable." I entered my uncle Albert's house more curious than anything else. I found myself standing in this very large foyer, and I could do nothing else but stare. Joseph broke the trance I was in, as he began to bring in my luggage. Uncle Albert directed Joseph to the room that I would be using every summer for next five years. After Joseph had brought everything in, my uncle invited me to follow him upstairs so I could see my room. I remember very clearly that my mind was going faster than I could digest the information. I had arrived at a very famous man's house, and it happened to be my uncle Albert's house, Albert Einstein to be exact.

Year Two of Discoveries

Before I go any further in my book of memoirs, I must share with my readers a most interesting story that took place on a warm and sunny day early in May.

My eyes opened to a most beautiful sunrise. It was the kind of sunrise you would see on a postcard or someone who is a talented photographer yet to be discovered. With so much energy in my body ready to burn, I hopped out of bed like an Olympic sprinter. Looking over my shoulder I could see the alarm clock, and it was coming up to six thirty. I remember saying to myself, "This is going to be a fine day." Little did I know that this day was going to be anything but fine and dandy.

Well, I better get on with this story before you get mad and throw the book at me. Excuse the pun. I brushed my teeth and hopped right into a hot shower. After getting dressed, I quickly proceeded downstairs to see if Uncle was up yet. As I walked into the kitchen, it looked empty, then all of a sudden I heard my uncle's voice coming from the pantry.

"Good morning, Stevie, did you sleep well?"

"Uncle, you scared the life out of me. I didn't know you were in the kitchen."

"Well, I have been accused of being as quite as a cat."

"Uncle, please don't do that again because it scares me."

"I am sorry. I will never do that again. Are you as hungry as I am, little one?"

"As a matter of fact, Uncle, I can eat a cow. What's on the menu, Uncle?"

"How about some scrambled eggs with toast and some nice ham slices with a side of fried potatoes.

Then, little one, we have to get to the laboratories. It's going to be a very busy day for me and possibly very interesting for you."

Let me tell you, it was a most glorious breakfast. We rinsed the dishes and neatly piled them in the sink, and off we went to the laboratories. It's only a five-minute walk to the entrance, where the guards check Uncle's ID and scan his body for anything foreign. We then proceeded to his office. Uncle put on his white lab coat, and he sat at his desk with a very serious grin, and then he looked up and stared into my face.

"Stevie, today is very top-secret work that we will be doing. I am going to allow you access to the testing area, but what you will be witnessing is never to be shared with anyone outside this building. Do you understand what I'm saying to you? I'm trusting you with knowledge that has everything to do with national security."

"I do understand everything you just told me, and no one will ever know what went on in here."

"Okay then, your word is good enough for me, Stevie."

My uncle went on to explain to me as basic as possible what went on back in the day. The scientist's goal was to cloak battleships with electromagnetic pulses. Therefore, the enemy could not see our battle cruisers, and you can't hit what you can't see. It was much more involved than that, but those are the basics. The team named their experiments the Philadelphia Project.

Apparently it all went haywire, and the ship disappeared with all hands on deck. You see, it worked so well that they couldn't bring the ship back with everyone on board. That's as much as I dare tell you. I was sworn to secrecy by my uncle, and in his memory, I won't say any more on this subject. If I do, I'll have to start killing my readers. I hope that my readers realize that I'm just kidding. Ha, ha, ha, got you.

I better get on with this story before all you readers get bored and shut the book. There is much more for you to discover. These memoirs are for the world to read and discover the real relationship between my uncle and me, and my hopes and desires are for you to see just what kind of man he really was. Keep in mind as you read on that he was a nonconformist and a true renegade to many of the government's ideas and decisions for the people of the United States. He was also extremely outspoken for what he believed in for all mankind. Unfortunately, with earth-shaking discoveries, the world didn't really appreciate what he has done for mankind. Maybe there will come a time in the distant future where civilization, if it does survive, will appreciate his work. Okay, enough of the theology lessons for now. Let me get back to that day in May where things got crazy in the laboratory, and they were about to get worse, a lot worse.

My uncle and I had a late lunch that day because of very involved experiments. By the time we finished, it had reached three o'clock. After returning from the men's room, my uncle looked at me with a very serious and worn face and said, "Little one, how about you and I go home for the day, I really have had it. Tomorrow is a new day and all of these experiments that are left to complete cannot be finished in one day. So how about you and I head for home?"

"That sounds like a great idea, Uncle, let's get out of here."

When we opened the double doors, we were greeted with a beautiful, sunny, and warm day. We began our walk back to Uncle's house, which, I said is a short distance from the laboratories. My uncle always held my hand when we went home at night as well as the morning.

For reasons that were never really clear to me until later on in life, my uncle never would walk on the sidewalks; instead he chose to walk in the street facing the oncoming traffic. I always felt that was pretty dangerous, but he always held my hand, and my position was on the inside, right next to the cars. All of a sudden, on this beautiful day in May, it happened. It happened so fast I wasn't prepared for it. It took me by complete surprise and scared the living shit out of me. We were on the way from a very exhausting day in the laboratories, especially for my uncle.

As I've said, it was a beautiful day in May, and we were walking along on the way to his house, and all of a sudden, I didn't feel my uncle's hand in mine anymore. I immediately stopped and looked around for my uncle. Suddenly I heard this gut-wrenching sound.

"Stevie, get me out of here."

When I came closer and closer to that sound, I must admit I was shocked. I didn't know whether to laugh or cry. When I looked down where my uncle's voice was coming from, he had stepped into a hole. The hole was an open manhole that wasn't covered up. He had fallen down about six feet to the bottom of the hole. Apparently the men were working on the road and forgot to close the hole with the manhole cover. They didn't even put up protective borders around the hole; they just walked away and left it open.

I tried the best I could to get him out, but to no avail. I started to scream to anyone who was within earshot. All of a sudden, there appeared a yellow truck with men in the back of it. They jumped off the back of the pickup and ran to my side. One of the men took a ladder out of the back of the truck and slid it down the hole. He then went and climbed down the ladder to my uncle and helped him climb to the surface.

When my uncle reached the surface, I almost didn't recognize him. Here was a little man climbing out of a manhole cover, and he looked as dirty as a chimney sweeper. He was covered from head to toe in black soot. For those who remember Al Jolson, the singer back in the day, that's what he looked like. When he finally was able to stand up, he definitely was not happy. But out of pure respect for my uncle, it took everything I had not to laugh. I remember very clearly as if it were yesterday. I just took his hand as we walked away, and all the men were saying how sorry they were that this incident had happened. My uncle didn't look back and certainly didn't respond to what they were saying.

Well, I'll tell you all, when we walked into his house, I didn't dare say anything to my uncle, probably because I really didn't know what to say, so I said nothing. That probably was the best single thing I could have done on that beautiful day in May.

The rest of that day was uneventful. We just hung around and didn't do much of anything. My uncle took a long hot shower, changed into some fresh clothes, then joined me in the kitchen.

"Stevie, considering that I could have been seriously hurt, how about we turn the day around and make a fantastic meal for ourselves."

"Well, Uncle, sounds good to me. What do you suggest?"

"I've been saving this beautiful rump roast in the freezer for a special occasion. This is the special occasion I was waiting for."

"Okay, Uncle, let's do it."

So after waiting for two hours, all the food was ready.

There was mashed potatoes, gravy, corn on the cob, and homemade bread that the housekeeper had given to my uncle a few days earlier. My uncle poured me a big glass of cold milk, and he poured himself a stemmed glass of one of his fine wines. We sat down and pigged out. It was one of the finest-tasting meals I had ever had. When we had finished, we just sat there and smiled at each other; we knew what the other was thinking. It was the best of times.

"Stevie, my little one, how would you like to play a game of Monopoly?"

I looked up at him with a big smile and asked if he still had that game. I thought he had thrown it away or given it away the year before.

"I saved it, just in case we might want to play more games. Tell you what, let's clean the kitchen, and then we can spread everything out on the table."

So that's exactly what we did. After the kitchen was clean, we spread everything out on the table and sat down to play a very competitive game of Monopoly. Even as a child with my young intelligence, I tended to be very competitive. But you know something, he was too. He played with vim and vigor. You would think he was trying to save the world with the passion by which he played. Well, the game went on for hours and hours, and we both lost track of time. We had to check to see what time it was. We had played for five hours, and it was almost 11:00 p.m. When he announced that, the five hours hit me quickly. I became very sleepy very fast. I told Uncle that I had had enough. We put everything away, and off to bed

I went. Oh, by the way, he beat me badly, but he usually did.

While at the laboratories on Friday, it rained all day and again on Saturday, and of course it rained all day on Sunday. When I opened my eyes on Monday morning, that beautiful sun was rising in the east, and the rays of the sun shined so brightly through the bedroom window, and I remember smiling and saying out loud, "That's what I'm talking about, another beautiful sunny day." After getting cleaned up, I went down to the kitchen, where I joined my uncle.

"Uncle, why is it you are always up so early every single day?"

"Stevie, that's a very good question. That deserves a very good answer. As we get older, we require fewer hours to sleep. As far as I know, the scientists don't know why. In fact, the best in their field of sleeping disorders still don't understand why we even have to sleep. I know it doesn't make any sense to you, Stevie, but in fact, it doesn't make any sense to me either. But if the theory holds true, you will require less and less sleep, as you get older."

There are a few things that most people don't even know about my uncle Albert. For instance, my uncle didn't care whether he wore the same colored socks or not; just as long as he was wearing socks, that was fine with him. To most levelheaded people, they would find this quite disturbing. As far as my uncle was concerned, it was fine. On the positive side, he loved to wear pullover sweaters with a button-down shirt. My uncle also loved to wear loafers when he could. He didn't wear them all the time because they hurt his feet. This was because he had flat feet like I do. Loafers didn't give him much support, so consequently they would hurt his feet. He also loved his collection of bowties, and let me tell you, he had quite the selection of them. My uncle had every color under the sun. He had solids, paisleys, and mixtures of the same colors, like shades of blue, gray, and even purple. Uncle Albert never wore a hat in his life. He believed that hats hurt the hair down to the roots. Let me tell you, if you don't know already, he had a full head of hair until the day he died. When it comes to me, I loved to wear loafers. My favorite color is blue, and I have never worn a hat. I am sixty-eight years old as I write these memoires, and I still have a full head of hair. Now, in my opinion, in a modern sense, I am better looking than my uncle was, but that is purely my opinion.

As you know, it was Monday morning, so we got ourselves together to walk to the laboratories. My uncle and I always walked hand in hand. It was such a wonderful feeling to be so close to my uncle. I felt so safe and content to have him as my uncle. There were many times I wished he was my father and not my uncle. Don't get me wrong, I was very grateful that Albert Einstein was my relative, and I had the opportunity to learn so many things from the man who was picked to be Man of the Century, the first man to ever be honored in that category. As long as I may live and being a writer, I don't know if I ever could find the words to express exactly how it felt to be the nephew of such a human being.

As we were walking towards the university, I finally decided it was time to ask the big question that had been on my mind for as long as I can remember. So I finally just spit it out, never really knowing what my uncle's reaction would really be.

"Uncle, tell me, what are we all about?"

Well, my uncle suddenly stopped right in his tracks. He turned around to face me and just stared at me, and then he spoke.

"Stevie, that question has been the topic of discussion by the most noted scientists in the world as long as I can remember. As of this date, we still don't have a definitive answer. There are many theories going around but still no exact answer. As long as you asked the question, you must also have a theory yourself."

"Uncle, I don't have the foggiest idea where we came from or how we came to be. If you believe in God's word, the Bible, then the answer is right in front of all of us. If one does not believe in the Bible, then they must believe in the big bang theory. Frankly, Uncle, I'm completely confused about the whole matter. Let's just forget I asked you the question. It's beginning to give me a bad headache. I guess that's a little too much for eight o'clock in the morning. I could use a stiff drink after asking you that question. Just kidding, Uncle."

"Would you do me a big favor, Stevie? Next time you ask me a question, how about you make it an easy one, like what's for dinner, okay?"

We arrived at the laboratories just after eight o'clock. While my uncle went for his cup of coffee, I went for my bottle of juice. I happen to love apple juice, but my favorite drink, believe it or not, is tomato juice. Most people don't realize that tomato juice has more vitamin C than orange juice does. The day was uneventful, and to tell you the truth, it was quite boring. You can't build an atomic bomb every day, ha ha ha.

Third Year of Discovery

To all my faithful readers, here is another extraordinary story from the years I spent with my uncle. Let me preface this event by saying, it is easier to believe fiction than a story like this.

As you very well know, every Sunday was soup day in the Einstein household; however, this Sunday was going to be remembered for a very, very long time. This little anecdote really explains the workings of my uncle in such a way that no one could possibly misunderstand the workings of his mind at times.

Without procrastinating the point, let's get right to it. As you know, it was soup day. On this particular Sunday, Uncle made beef vegetable soup, which, by the way, was absolutely out of this world. It had everything in it but the kitchen sink. Well, after two bowls of the vitamin-filled delicacy, it was time to rinse the dishes and put them in the sink. Oh, by the way, my uncle would make the most delicious bread on Sunday mornings to go with soup of the day.

As I was finishing the dishes, Uncle announced that he was going to take his shower. I continued doing what I was doing to clean up when I heard this god-awful screaming. I initially thought that my uncle had turned on the TV or radio. Well, I was wrong on both accounts. The screaming continued, so I decided to follow the harsh interruption to its source. I approached the loud sounds and was totally confused. The sounds were coming from inside the clothes closet. "Get me out of here, Stevie, right now!" The voice belted out again. I instinctively tried to open the closet door, but it would not open. A second or so later, I gave it everything I had in my upper body. The door opened, and when it did, the force propelled me backward over the top of Uncle's couch and onto the floor. When I looked up, there was Uncle standing over me with a big grin on his face.

"Are you okay, Stevie?"

"Just fine, Uncle. I guess I'm stronger than I thought I was. What in the world happened to you, Uncle?"

"I guess I went into the clothes closet to take a shower. Now that's not smart, Stevie. The next time it could be dangerous to my health."

The rest of the day was uneventful for both of us. After we both cleaned up, it was time to go to the pond for a while. So Uncle filled a basket of fresh fruit, and off we went to see the mother ducks and their babies. So that was the Sunday that never was in the beginning of the third year of discovery. We, of course, never talked about that incident ever again, and no one was ever the wiser.

Now, for all you readers, enough of the fun and games. We are going to move to the dark side of things. What most people don't realize, and it's not their fault, is I know things about my uncle that the world doesn't know, and it's about time you read about these facts.

There was something about the duck pond that was very relaxing and at the same time very cathartic for my uncle Albert. He would admit the deepest, darkest secrets and his innermost feelings to me.

On one beautiful sunny day at the pond, he started crying, and it was very shocking to me. This strong-willed but very modest and humble man was shedding tears in front of me. I didn't know exactly what to say at first, so I waited. Then very cautiously, I asked him if he was all right. He looked up at me and paused and began to share with me why he was crying.

"Stevie, there are four areas of my life that I regret and am very remorseful about.

"The first area of regret is my manic depression. I never knew where it came from or who gave it to me, but it has caused immeasurable problems in my everyday life. Sometimes I find myself in hell, and then there are times I'm the happiest person in the world. Then there are times I am in both places, and

I truly don't know if I am coming or going. Stevie, there are times I can't even eat. My weight goes up and down like the sun rising and falling every day.

"Stevie, take the laboratory work for instance. One minute I'm happy and kidding with my colleagues, and the next minute I'm chewing them out. Little one, like I have said, sometimes I don't know if I'm coming or going.

"Now, take sleeping for example. Sometimes I wake up with a bad headache, sometimes in a good mood, and sometimes in a really angry state of mind. The ironic part about it is, sometimes I actually wonder if I'm going insane, and sometimes it scares the living shit out of me.

"There are days I have such bad stomach pains and loose bowels because of it. This and much more have been going on for as long as I can remember. Maybe that's why I smoke so much, because I am so nervous wondering what's going to come next in my life."

"Uncle, I've never seen you cry before. Is there anything I can do to make you feel better?"

"No, little Stevie, it's just something I have to live with until the day I die. But I can honestly tell you it's one of the hardest things I've ever had to cope with."

"Uncle, haven't you always taught me to take one day at a time? You have also shared with me on more than one occasion that one foot in front of another gets you where you want to go. I've come to believe it, and more importantly, I've come to make it part of my everyday practice."

"You are right, little one. Isn't it ironic that you are reminding me of what I've been teaching you? You are a very good student, my little one."

"But, Uncle, don't forget you are a great teacher."

"Thank you, you have made me feel much better for saying that to me. You are a very loving little boy with a very advanced mind."

"Of course, Uncle. Just look at where I came from, not to mention my genealogy. Uncle, I can ruin everything I've been given if I don't use my own talents that God has blessed me with."

"Stevie, how did you get so wise for being so young?"

"Well, Uncle, I can ask you the same question. Furthermore, I believe if you want the best truth there is at any given moment, all one has to do is look at themselves in the mirror, and what comes back at them is the best truth they're ever going to see."

"Stevie, you're a little boy with a large capacity for understanding, and you make my hairs on my spine stand up, and I get chills just listening to you."

"Coming from you, Uncle, that is an extreme compliment, thank you very much."

"No, Stevie, thank you."

"Now, Uncle, before you get to the other categories of remorse, how about we fix some lunch to energize us?"

"Stevie, that sounds like a great idea to me. Remember the meat loaf I made yesterday, Stevie? How would you like a cold meat loaf sandwich, little one?"

"I love meat loaf, Uncle, I would love one."

"Okay, then afterwards we will talk further about my other regrets in life, Stevie."

"That was delicious, Uncle. We have to do that again real soon."

"Now, Stevie, how about we go into the living room and get comfortable so I can describe the second regret of my life."

"Okay, Uncle, lead the way."

"Okay, Stevie, the second regret of my life was being a very bad husband and father to my children. I guess I should have known that I wasn't one to get married, but I did. I wasn't very faithful to my first wife, not to mention I was a very bad father spending very little time with my children. It was always work, work, work, never truly realizing that there is more to life than my head stuck in a book. If I would have really been honest with myself at the time, it would have been as plain as the glasses on my face that the more time I spent away from my wife and family, the more I was drifting further and further away from them. I know it happens to many married couples, but it was happening in my life, and I guess, the truth be known, I really didn't care enough to correct what was happening at the time.

"The beginning of my downfall as a husband started at the laboratories. I would work later and later, and that alone drove my wife and me further and further apart. But that wasn't the worst of it. There were very pretty assistants that worked around me, and I've always known from a very early age that I like girls too much. What really happened was I became a flirt, then I graduated to an all-out womanizer, and that was the beginning of the end for me and my marriage. Two things eventually happened with my first wife. She fell out of love with me, and she heard rumors of my cheating on her. When she approached me about it, I really couldn't lie any further about my sexual encounters. It was all over. Truth be known, what really hurt me about my divorce was not the divorce itself but hurting my children the way I did. In hindsight, I never should have had children in the first place. In fact, I never should have gotten married ever. But in life, my little one, you live and learn. Let this be a good lesson for your future. Be damn sure that the decisions you make in life are ones that you can live with for your whole life. Try never to have too many regrets in life, and you will have a reasonably happy life. Do you understand what I'm saying to you? Good, little one, then this is a great lesson you have learned today, one that I promise will last you a lifetime. Now, how would you like to go out for ice cream and on to the park? Do you think it's a good idea?"

"Uncle, that's the best idea I've heard today!"

"Then, little one, how about we get ready and go have some fun feeding the ducks and their babies learning to swim."

We had a quiet walk to the pond, and it was very enjoyable. The weather couldn't have been more perfect. The sun was bright overhead, and the birds were singing their messages to one another. We were able to find a bench right in front of the ducks that were performing for each other.

"Say, Uncle, can we talk about the third topic of remorse that you keep so deeply inside?"

"Yes, my little one, we shall continue."

"The third topic of remorse is creating, inventing, or whatever you wish to label it, the theory of relativity, E=MC². The day I birthed that formula, I was going to the bathroom. If I would have been aware of what they, the scientific world, and the government were going to do with it, I would have taken the formula, which I squiggled on toilet paper, and flushed it down the toilet."

"I don't understand what you mean, Uncle. The statement you just made to me makes no sense whatsoever."

"Of course it doesn't. I need to start at the very beginning, little one.

"In the beginning, when I created the theory of relativity in the bathroom, I simultaneously realized it wasn't one item that made up the formula, it was several different categories. One of those categories was energy. If everything else was in order, everything is relative to itself. What I'm trying to tell you is that for every action, there is an opposite and equal reaction. By splitting the atom and creating fusion, there would be never-ending energy on the planet Earth. For example, submarines could be fitted with radioactive material to keep them moving indefinitely. Another example of never-ending energy would be electricity, which would produce heat and lights for everyone to use globally.

"Now, little Stevie, I'm going to jump a little ahead in this story to show you the remorse and guilt I've had to live with.

"From the creation of the atom, it led to the building of the two atomic bombs that were dropped in 1945, one on Hiroshima and one bomb on Nagasaki. One hundred thousand human beings were vaporized instantly. Millions, after that, died from radiation poisoning. I've had to live with the fact that I was responsible for the death of millions. I ask you, little one, how would you like that knowledge on your mind when you're trying to go to sleep. The men and women, the children, the future children, and most certainly the grandparents of the children destroyed—all destroyed. Do you get the picture, Stevie?"

I looked down at the ground; I guess it was because of such extreme sadness that I had felt. I then answered my uncle's question. I looked up at my uncle and told him that I understood everything that he had just told me. If I could have seen my facial expression at that moment, I'm sure it would have been an expression that I never could have explained.

"Eventually my ideas were realized, and that is how the Manhattan Project came about. That project was in fact the most guarded secret in recorded history. No one outside of the people working on it ever knew it even existed. I was asked to head up the project probably because I was the one most likely to succeed.

"At different stages of the project, the intensity of the bomb was tested, but we never actually tested the bomb itself. No one on the project really knew if the bomb would really work until they were dropped from the B-52. Once the bombs were dropped out of the bay doors of the B-52, they were set to explode at ten thousand feet. Fortunately, they did what they were supposed to. The bottom line of this whole nightmare is that I have never been able to let it go. To dismiss it from my mind has been beyond my capabilities, and that's the bottom line of this nightmare."

"Uncle, how have you been able to live with all of this?"

"That's easy to answer, little one. I haven't, and being totally truthful with myself, I don't think I will ever get over it. Now, I think that's enough honesty for one day. What do you say about making some dinner?"

"Right about now, Uncle, that sounds like a great idea. That dinner was delicious and very filling. Has anyone ever told you that you are a very good cook?"

"Not lately, little one, but thank you for the compliment. How about we leave the dishes right where they are and go sit in the living room so I can finish the last category of remorse?

"The last category of remorse has to do with your father, my half-brother. For longer than I like to remember, he has literally hated me. I'm not sure I fully understand that concept of hate.

"I guess in my own way, I have been very successful, but so has your father. It is true, I won the Nobel Peace Prize in 1929, and he didn't. It is also true that I discovered the theory of relativity, he didn't.

Furthermore, it is also true I went on to contribute much to physics and the world of science, space, and time, and he didn't. Finally, it was with those discoveries, that we were able to stop World War II.

"Now, little one, let's examine what your father has accomplished. From a very early age Alfred new what he wanted to do: he wanted to own companies. So he started with a little diner and went on to own many diners. Then, when that was a success, he started buying delicatessens. In fact, he loved them so much he bought ten of them. It wasn't too long before all of them were doing just fine. I remember very clearly he always said that location, location, location had made them a total success. Of course, there are other reasons that must be in place to make anything a success. I also remember very clearly Alfred telling me that if you don't hurt their wallets in the process, they will be back. Alfred went on to own an importing/exporting business of eggs, cheeses, and other specialized products.

"In fact, my brother went on to own twenty-seven companies. If that wasn't enough, he went to a place called Glens Falls, New York, and had built a monstrous log cabin called Alfred's Restaurant. It seated five hundred people at one time, and the place looked gorgeous. Being his last accomplishment, he knew it had to be a big success, and believe me, it was. The point of this comparison between him and me is not for bragging purposes but to show you that we were both successful in something. Your father, Stevie, was a billionaire when you were born in 1945.

"What do you think of that?"

"Pretty impressive, Uncle."

"Now, I would like for you to explain to me why he hated me so much."

"I can't, Uncle, I can't explain this to you. I don't know how to."

"Stevie, this remains a mystery to me for all these decades, and I am very remorseful about that."

Fourth Year of Discovery

It's now the beginning of April 1953, and I am looking forward with a great amount of anxiety to get the hell out of this prison for another six months of fresh air in Princeton.

I don't blame my father or my uncle for the disease I inherited from them. This ugly disease called bipolar stayed hidden in me until I was thirty-eight years old, and then all hell broke loose one day, and I was never the same anymore. I guess, truth be known, I still love my father and uncle in spite of my damn luck. Consequently, when I had a daughter in my twenties, it passed to her, and that's something that's very difficult for me to live with.

However, life goes on whether we want it to or not. You should also know that even after decades, my daughter has never forgiven me for that little surprise she woke up with one morning.

Over the last few years, I have grown very close to my uncle Albert. He is so different in many ways than most people I have ever met. Even though my father and he are half-brothers, they are as different as night and day. Even though they are brilliant in their own ways, they are enemies to this day. They don't write, they don't call each other, and to my knowledge, they have not seen each other in decades.

In a few days I'll be leaving for Princeton, and I can't wait to see my uncle again. For reasons that were never really clear to me, I get along with my uncle like two peas in a pod. When I first met Uncle, we hit it off right away. We bonded like we had known each other for a lifetime. He was a very small man in stature, but a giant on planet Earth. After Uncle died in 1955, they studied his brain to try and determine the difference between his brain and others. Guess what?

There was not one difference of any kind between his brain and anyone else. To this day, as I write these memoirs, no one has discovered Albert Einstein's secret to why his brain was different than anyone else on this planet.

The night before I was to leave for Princeton, there was a knock at my bedroom door. In walked my father with a big smile on his face. Emotionally, I must have stepped back ten feet, wondering what my father had on his mind. Even though he had bipolar disease, he could be very lucid at times and a great father to be with.

"Stevie, how would you like to have dinner with me tonight, and then you can call your uncle on the eve of your trip to Princeton."

"Dad, I think that is a great idea, and I would really like that."

Well, I had a great talk with my uncle, and after our talk, I was even more excited to get on the road to Princeton. After dinner I disappeared into my room to get ready for the next morning.

My night didn't exactly go the way I wanted. I tossed and turned, probably because there was too much on my mind. To say the least, I was more excited to get out of the restaurant and on the road than just seeing my uncle.

Somewhere around four o'clock in the morning, I had had it with tossing and turning, so I got up and just sat on the edge of my bed and just let my mind wander. All of a sudden, I realized that I was hungry. I didn't care what time it was; it was time to open up the big kitchen and start cooking.

I put on my bathrobe and slippers, and off I went into the huge kitchen located in the back of the restaurant. When it came to breakfast, I usually cooked the same things. My breakfast consisted of four scrambled eggs and some kind of meats, usually roast beef and turkey. After cutting up the two meats and adding it into the scrambled eggs, it was time to add the dried noodles. Now, the dried noodles were for a little crunch; it added a little kick to it. The last item to add was a little milk to make the eggs fluffy. I buttered a large frypan, emptied everything into it, and just sat back and watched it all cook on a small flame. The smell was intoxicating.

After eating all of that fantastic food, I washed it down with a large glass of cold milk. I felt like a new person and I also felt I could conquer the entire world. So, it was time to rinse all the dishes and frying pans that I had used. Once that was done, it was time to get the hell out of the kitchen. The reason for that was because my evil, evil stepmother would be getting up, followed by my mafia father, and I didn't want any kind of confrontation with either one of them. I was in a great mood with a full stomach and was ready to get showered and dressed in contemplation of getting on the road to Princeton.

I found God at a very young age, and I am so grateful I did. Unlike other children, I had no childhood to talk of. I was made to wash dishes, floors, and bathrooms in the restaurant. Now that I am almost sixty-nine, writing these memoirs, I am not complaining—not at all. If I were to thank my father for anything, it would be that he taught me to do a great job no matter what that job may be, and second, he taught me never to give up no matter how hard something is. Furthermore, he made me tough. In other words, I could accomplish anything if I really wanted to. For all of those things and a few more that I will not discuss at this time, I will always be grateful to my dad. I loved him completely, no matter what he had turned into. I loved him till the day he died. I just didn't like him as a person or a father. That being said, it's time to get back to the story.

By the time I showered and got dressed, it was approaching nine o'clock, and I knew everyone was up and working to open the restaurant. I walked out into the kitchen and said good morning to my evil, evil stepmother and my Mafioso father. I was especially nice to both of them so as not to cause any problems for the simple reason that I would be leaving for Princeton in a few minutes, and I wanted to stay in a good mood. All of a sudden, Joseph walked into the kitchen, and I was extremely happy to see him. He had a few items to go over with my father, and then he turned to me and said, "Master Stephen, are you ready to get on the road?"

I looked up at him and said, "You bet your life I am."

Joseph and I said good-bye to everyone and walked out to the limo. I got in the front seat, where I liked to sit. Joseph put all my luggage in the trunk, and off we went. I couldn't have been happier to leave that property.

Being spring, the temperature was still very comfortable, and the sky was so blue. We talked every now and then, nothing too heavy or involved. You see, he knew I had a very bad relationship with my stepmother and not-so-good relationship with my dad.

By the time we reached the outskirts of New York City, we were always very hungry, and as you know, Joseph and I always stopped at the same diner. We had eaten there several times before and always enjoyed the food. So we stopped there once again. Joseph let me out at the front door, as he always did, and proceeded to park the limo.

We walked in to a very busy diner this time but got seated at a booth within a few minutes. "Joseph," I said, "I can eat a horse!" Joseph looked at me and, in a very rare moment, agreed with exactly what I had said to him. Joseph did caution me about how much food to order. He didn't want my head to be hungrier than my stomach.

Joseph and I had a great meal, as usual; he paid the bill, and off we went.

Actually, from this point on the map, we weren't very far from Princeton. I was really getting excited to see my uncle, whom I hadn't seen in seven months even though I had talked to him on the phone several times during that period. We ran into a lot of traffic as we entered New Jersey. However, Joseph made good time, and at about five o'clock, we rolled into my uncle's driveway. I don't know how my uncle does it, I mean, timing our trip, but he was outside waiting for us to pull up to the front door. The car no sooner came to a stop, then I jumped out and ran to my uncle. I gave him a big hug and kiss and told him how happy I was to see him and be in New Jersey. Believe or not, I really felt I was home, where I should really be. My uncle and I went inside while Joseph brought in my luggage and deposited it in my room on the second floor. It has been decades since that time but I still remember how it felt when I sat down on uncle's couch; I let out a big breath followed by a very big smile on my face. Yes, I was really home again, home where I should be, home where I should have been for the last nine years of my life.

There were many times in my life as I got older that I had wished my uncle had been my father. There is no doubt whatsoever, had it been that way, my life would have been much different. To give you an example, if my uncle would have been my father, there is no doubt that I would have gone on to graduate high school and then on to college. Actually, there were two vocations that really interested me. First, I wanted to become a doctor so as to help many hurting people. If I didn't become a doctor, I wanted to become a lawyer and defend people in court that I felt were innocent. But life takes strange turns sometimes, and what you think will happen, doesn't. Anyway, I didn't turn out so bad. I have never been in trouble with the law, never in prison or jail, never drank or gambled, and I have a perfect driving record. So as you can see, I've done good things in my life. There is one more thing that I think is very important: I've worked all my life and paid the taxes that I am supposed to; what I mean to say is that I have never been in trouble with the IRS.

Now, I better get on with the story before you readers close my book and put it on a shelf to get dusty.

As always, Joseph stayed and visited with my uncle for a few minutes before he took off for the return trip home. Even though it was approaching six o'clock, he should make it back to the restaurant by nine or ten tonight.

After Joseph left, my uncle asked me if I was hungry even though he knew the answer. He made a magnificent dinner of steak and mashed potatoes with mixed vegetables. To say the least, it was delicious, and of course, I ate more than I should have, but that's what I do. After dinner, we cleaned up the kitchen and went out into the living room to talk.

"Stevie, tomorrow we are doing some testing in the laboratories, and I do believe that these tests will be of great interest to you. So I want you in bed by nine o'clock so you have an opportunity to get a good night's sleep. How does that sound to you?"

"Uncle, that's a plan," I answered.

I slept like a little baby, and actually I was up and showered before my uncle was. When he walked into the kitchen, I was already there.

"Good morning, Uncle, I slept fantastic."

"Good job, Stevie. What we are going to do in the laboratory is top secret, and I know I can count on you to keep it secret."

"What kind of tests will you be doing that are so secret?"

"Well, you will just have to wait to find out what we will be doing."

After breakfast, we had a nice walk to the laboratories; while uncle was conferring with his assistants, I sat quietly at his desk, waiting to be called. Looking around the laboratory, I discovered new equipment had been installed since the last time I had been there. It's strange, but at a very young age I found out that one of my many abilities to come was the ability to remember anything I looked at. My uncle once told me it was a form of a photographic memory. Later on in my life, it got stronger and stronger; I mean the ability to remember anything I wanted to and the ability to recall it anytime I wished to. As I have gotten older, that particular talent has served me well in life.

After a few minutes, uncle joined me at his desk. He pulled up another chair and started to explain what was going to happen with these sets of tests.

"Stevie, what we are going to attempt to do is change the molecular makeup of a certain object and move it from one place to another. If it works, it will be the beginning of teleportation. It's eventual use will revolutionize travel and transportation. It could change the space program entirely for long voyages to distant planets. Stevie, you must understand, what happens in this laboratory stays in this laboratory. Do I make myself perfectly clear?"

"Uncle, I understand exactly what you're saying, and you have my word that what happens in this facility is a question of national security. Am I correct, Uncle, in saying that?"

"I couldn't have said it better if I tried, Stevie."

When the tests began, I was given special goggles to wear to protect my eyes. They were much bigger than my size, but I secured them by holding them against my face with my two hands. The combination of different waves changed the molecular makeup of the object; however, it did not move the object to it's final resting place, which was on the opposite side of the room. Not only did it not move the object, but it changed the object into a different shape. The test was a complete failure. If this theoretical test of mass can be accomplished, the application to mankind and the way we live will be astounding. My uncle was disappointed but not nearly done. "That is the way it goes sometimes, Stevie, trial and error, one foot in front of the other, gets you where you want to go."

After a very long and disappointing day at the laboratory, we walked home to a delicious dinner and a game of checkers. As I was heading to bed, he turned to me and said something I will always remember, "Tomorrow is another day, Stevie. Just remember, you always have another crack at it. Never, never give up on anything you want to attain. Just take a step back, take a deep breath, and look at the problem again. You will see it differently, and you will try again and again till you succeed. Giving up is not an option. Do you understand what I've told you?" I will never forget this lesson. From that time forward until presently, I have never forgotten his words of wisdom, and I never will.

Before I knew it, spring had turned into summer. Time was flying by too fast. My uncle and I had so many good times together that year. We took bike trips on ready-made paths. Of course, we enjoyed numerous times at the pond with the new baby ducks learning how to swim from the mama duck. There were many nights of checkers, which I enjoyed so very much, and, of course, many terrific meals that Uncle made.

Finally, to my dismay, it was September and time to pack up and leave till next April. In hindsight, thinking back on my fourth year of discovery, I learned so much from my uncle Albert. There was so much knowledge given to me by my uncle that it will last me a lifetime, and so far it has.

As I walked away to the waiting limo, my uncle made the comment that I had a lot in store for me next spring. He also told me that it would be a year of fantastic discovery, a year I would never forget as long as I live.

Fifth and Final Year of Discovery

Shortly after I arrived home from my uncle's, I became ten years old. I was still a young boy with a very advanced mind. There wasn't much I couldn't do. Oh, I almost forgot, I couldn't drive on the highway, but I could do most anything else. My birthday passed uneventfully, and before I knew it, we were way into fall. Every year that I went to my uncle's, I began to get excited once we were through with winter. This particular winter was rough. There was a great amount of snow and ice and especially subzero weather.

We finally arrived at the March winds, and believe it or not, I was excited. In less than a month, I would be packing up and getting ready to leave for Princeton, New Jersey.

I think the last eight months passed really fast because I purposely kept myself as busy as I could. When I wasn't washing dishes or cleaning bathrooms, I would love to read. I loved trivia, adventures, and even books of science fiction. Truthfully, by the time I was ten, I had read quite extensively. I really don't know how many hundreds of books I had finished by the time spring had sprung.

It was 1955, and I truly believed great things were going to happen to me. I had no real proof, mind you, but it was an overwhelming feeling in that direction. This year was going to be one of great discoveries. Exactly what discoveries, I couldn't tell you, but the feelings were that overwhelming nevertheless. I think you get my drift.

Once again, for the fifth year, Irene packed all of my clothes for the trip to my uncle's. It finally dawned on me one sunny day that I thought she packed me up with a big smile on her face, simple because she was happy to get rid of me. Believe it or not, she was jealous of my father's love for me. Irene had no reason to be jealous because my relationship with my father was a love-hate relationship, and there was absolutely nothing to be jealous about. My father did love Irene very much and he was very good to her.

Well, enough of the dreariness.

The morning finally arrived for Joseph to check the limo out completely and fill the twenty-five-gallon tank up. As usual and, may I say, quite promptly, Joseph appeared in the kitchen, and I said my fond good-byes. Ha ha ha! And then off we went.

The time flew bye as fast as the Concorde jet that flies at 100,000 feet at speeds that exceed 1,200 miles per hour. Before I knew it, we were at our favorite diner. As usual, we were both very hungry, so hungry I could have ordered one item from column A and one item from column B. But seriously if it wasn't for Joseph, I probably would have.

The traffic was horrendous, and we were not making very good time. It was getting dark by the time we had reached the outskirts of New York City.

As we entered New Jersey, we ran into another bottleneck. If that wasn't bad enough, we then ran into a police checkpoint. That's where they check your license, registration, insurance card, tires, and anything else they wished to bother you about.

We had finally reached the head of the line where the police started to check our limo; when something very odd happened. We were told to pull off to the side of the road and wait for another police officer.

All of a sudden, Joseph turned to me and asked me to pull down the visor that held the mirror. He then asked me to open the mirror and look in the backseat. When I did as he asked, my face must have turned white followed by a very big gasp.

I turned my face directly in front of his and just stared.

"Stevie, do you see what I see?"

"Joseph, there is another person in the backseat!"

I immediately turned back and once again looked into the mirror. There he was, still sitting there. I remember blinking my eyes a couple of times just to clear my eyesight. It made no difference. The image of a young boy still appeared sitting in the backseat. I whipped my whole body around to face this image head on.

I could hardly talk, but I finally managed to get something out of my mouth.

"Who are you, and where did you come from?"

At first, whoever it was did not answer me, then this image spoke to me.

"You are about to take a journey that only a very few have taken. You are one of the chosen ones. I am making myself visible to you, by the highest powers. You are to follow your uncles' directions and believe what he has to say to you. Furthermore, he will be your only guide to the universe; never betray. You are one of the chosen ones. Never betray your new found knowledge. The cost of betrayal may be more than you can pay. Your guide to the universe will be Professor Albert Einstein. You will be asked never to reveal the contents of this journey while Professor Einstein is alive. From that point on, it will be left up to your discretion when and where to reveal what you know. Are you in agreement with these terms I have laid out, Stevie?"

"Whoever you are, I am not sure I fully understand what you have said. But if it has to do with my uncle Albert, I agree with your terms on that basis."

I turned to look at Joseph for just a second. When I turned back to look at my visitor, he was gone as fast as he had appeared.

I turned back to Joseph once again and asked, "What just happened, Joseph? What just happened to us?"

"Are we hallucinating Joseph? Or maybe we're losing our minds. Are we insane or is the world?"

"I don't know, Stevie," he answered with a very puzzled look on his face.

Then, all of a sudden, a policeman appeared at Joseph's window. He asked us to get out of the limo and stand on the side of the road. He further went on to order Joseph to open the trunk. Joseph did as he was told, and once the trunk was inspected, we were told that we could go on our way, and we did just that! In fact, we hauled ass.

For the balance of the trip to Princeton, we didn't say a word to each other, not one word. We pulled into Uncle's driveway about nine o'clock and found Uncle waiting outside for us as he had always done in the past.

The limo no sooner stopped, then I ran from the car and gave my uncle one big hug and kiss, not daring to say one word of what happened on the way to see him. I was just happy to arrive and be in the arms of his love. I was home, home where I should have always been.

While my uncle and I got settled inside, Joseph brought my luggage into the house and deposited them neatly in my room. He then came downstairs and joined in with our conversation while my uncle went and got us all a cold drink.

From the look on Joseph's face, I could clearly see that Joseph was happy for me, and Joseph knew beyond a shadow of a doubt that I was really home. We sat and talked for the longest time. Then Joseph got up and announced that he better hit the road. He wanted to be home by breakfast to eat with Josephine, his wife and my nanny. I gave Joseph a big hug and kiss, and then he was gone. I wouldn't be seeing him for another six months. As always, I will miss seeing and talking to him like I do every day. Then Uncle and I went to bed. Like Uncle always says, tomorrow is another day, and one step in front of another gets you where you want to go. I was so tired and yet totally confused at what had happened to Joseph and me on the road. And come to think of it, I never did tell my uncle about that mysterious incident that scared the shit out of me at the road check with the police standing right outisde the car. Finally, I drifted off in a deep, deep sleep with an empty mind for the time being. However, unbeknownst to me, the scariest times were yet to come, and I wouldn't have to wait too long.

I woke up the next morning feeling very tired, probably because I didn't get any quality sleep. I put my robe on and went downstairs to the kitchen. My uncle was already cooking his famous breakfast of eggs, toast, ham, and sausage, and my ice-cold milk was waiting for me in the refrigerator.

"Sit down, Stevie, breakfast is just about to be served. I wondered when you were going to get up. If you didn't come downstairs in the next ten minutes, I would have come upstairs to wake you. But you were kind enough to save me a trip.

"After breakfast, let's get showered and dressed and walk over to the pond and see the little babies. How about it?"

"You know, Uncle, that sounds great to me. Let's do that."

After spending a few hours at the pond, talking and watching the new babies, we took a slow walk back to the house. We just sat around talking about this and that, nothing too important. Before we knew it, the clock was about to strike two o'clock, and believe it or not, we were hungry again. You know, it's just like going camping; you are always hungry, probably because of the fresh air.

The rest of April went pretty fast, and April turned into May, and May turned into June. According to the weather, summer was here, and my life was just about to take a left-hand turn into the dark zone. My uncle was just about to hurtle me so far into the darkness and coldness of space that my life would never be the same again, ever. All of this was to begin in the latter part of August.

The sun rose in perfect harmony with Mother Nature on August 25. I had a fantastic night's sleep, and I was ready to take on the world. After showering and getting dressed, I went downstairs and headed right for the kitchen. It wasn't any big surprise that my uncle was there, cooking another one of his delicious breakfasts.

"Good morning, Uncle," I said with all the gusto in my little frame of a body. He turned and just gave me a big smile that went from one side of his face to another. He very rarely ever did that, but I didn't give it much thought at the time. Later on that day, I found out what that rather large smile had really meant.

After finishing another one of Uncle's fantastic breakfasts, we rinsed the dishes and neatly stacked them on the counter. Then, Uncle turned to me and asked if I would mind going into the living room; he needed to talk with me about something very important.

"Stevie, I would like us to go to the park today because there are important subjects I need to discuss with you. Is that okay with you?"

"Uncle, that's the best idea I've heard today. Sure, I'd love to go and see the ducks and their babies."

"Well, Stevie, that's not what I had in mind exactly. Everything will be explained when we get there."

We took a slow walk to the park, only we didn't sit by the ducks. My uncle looked for a very secluded place to sit.

"Stevie, I want to talk with you about something very important. My little one, you are one of only a few people that I trust. What I am about to discuss with you must never go any further than this bench. Everything I need to tell you will take a few visits to the park. The reason we go to the park little one, is because I believe my house is being bugged. I also believe the government is the one doing it. Furthermore, I believe that they can't take any chances with me. Truth be known they don't trust me. Do I have your solemn word you will never reveal anything we talk about here?"

"Of course, Uncle, you have my solemn oath never to discuss anything you don't want repeated."

"There is one more item that I want to make perfectly clear to you. You are not to discuss any of this most secretive information while I'm alive. After I'm gone, I really don't give a damn what you repeat. Is this perfectly clear, Stevie?"

"I understand exactly what you have told me, and I will do exactly what you've said. You have my word."

"That's good enough for me, Stevie. First of all, let's return to Egypt, over three thousand years ago. If you think that the Egyptians build those pyramids all by themselves, you don't know how wrong you would be. They had lots of help from an unlikely source.

"Actually, it was the Egyptians who were the ones to first meet the aliens up close and personal. The Egyptians believed they were gods and they even spoke our language.

"The construction of the pyramids did start with many thousands of workers, but when the aliens landed, they had a new kind of technology to help them, technology that amazed the Egyptians. In fact, the Egyptians never knew that they even existed. How could they have known? The aliens' planet is millions of miles away from our galaxy, which, as you know, is the Milky Way galaxy. Because of their technology, it was not difficult to transport the huge blocks of stone that were used to build the pyramids from the quarries to the building sites. If you think they were transported by the Egyptian boats, you would be wrong again. The stones themselves had to be mined at the quarries, transported quite a ways to the boats, then brought quite a ways to the site of the pyramids. They didn't have many boats, and the distance to the sites of the pyramids were many miles away. Hypothetically, it would take thousands of years to build any kind of pyramid. One of the guarded secrets was that they were equipped with gravitational fields that actually picked up these huge stones and transported them to the sites. It is true, however, that there were masons that cut the stones into the square shapes and sizes that were needed.

"Now, let's talk about the Sphinxes. Unbeknownst to even modern science, the reason they look so perfect is because they were cut by laser from their ships above, then transported to the desired sites. In fact, the statues that stood in front of the temples were cut by the aliens according to the Achitect's drawing showing height, width and any markings wanted. Then, they too were transported to the desired sites in front of the temples.

"The aliens were very impressed with Egyptians' way of life and their demeanor. Furthermore, they were more than happy to assist them. Mainly because the aliens were not hostile in any way and they were here on missions of peace and to show their good faith.

"Even before the Egyptians, the cavemen have pictures of the small crafts and little people that looked like spacemen drawn on cave walls all over the world.

"Stevie, this is enough for one day. We will return tomorrow, same time, same place, and I will talk to you about the moon, Mars, and beyond. Let's go home and eat."

The rest of the day went great. We just hung around the house and nibbled on this and that and played checkers. When I was sick of losing at checkers, we changed to monopoly. As usual, I lost at that too. My uncle happens to be very good at board games. Why? I don't have the answer; he just is.

I'm sure all of my readers do realize that we only went to the park on the weekends. I must admit, Uncle did know how to relax; most people don't, once they're out of work for the day or weekend.

We both went to bed fairly early Saturday night, but we slept well. On Sunday morning, my uncle made his usual array of food for breakfast and spread it out from one end of the table to the other. Once we cleared the table and rinsed all the dishes, off we went to our secret place at the pond.

Whether our scientists are just stupid or enjoy spending all of our money for ridiculous projects still remains to be seen. So far, they are just stupid, according to my uncle. They continue to study the moon, Mars, and beyond. They are all looking in the wrong place.

First of all, the moon is a dead body of useless rock, good to no one. It doesn't even hold any future for mining minerals. That is because there isn't any to mine. In the future, if there is one, the only good purpose that the moon would serve is a jumping off place to get to other planets and galaxies. However, to do that, there has to be a colony established there to live and produce some kind of fossil fuel and a refueling method to power our galactic ships to go anywhere they want. So far, that is many years away, if at all, my uncle states to me. The scientists theory and it is fully believable is that there was never any kind of life on the moon at any time; even in the context of colonies living there. My uncle assures me right from the horse's mouth that the moon has given forth nothing to benefit earthlings in any way, or anyone else, ever. The moon is just there, like your appendix or your spleen. We can do without it in our bodies because it serves no real purpose to us.

When we talk about mars, that's a different subject altogether. Mars seems to have polar caps that have existed for maybe millions of years. According to the aliens my uncle has talked to, the planet Mars has never been populated. The aliens, in fact, look some what like us. They are distinctly taller and dress much differently than us. Their skulls are larger than ours, and the reason for that is because they have unusually large brains. Our scientists have stated that we use maybe 7 to 10 percent of our brain power, for lack of a better word. They use almost 100 percent of their brain power. They are millions of years ahead of us, and they come from distant planets far beyond our galaxy.

Our SETI program, which stands for Search for Extraterrestrial Intelligence, is a joke. The simple reason for that is because we don't have the technology to cover all the area necessary to find any life, not to mention the long-reaching ability to hear any sounds beyond our galaxy.

According to my uncle and certain others, we are not alone. Life on other planets really exists, it's just that we can't reach them yet, and if that is ever possible, it will be a very long time and far into the future of mankind. With all of that being said, my uncle and I went out to eat at one of his favorite watering holes that had nothing but buffet. It was surely, another great day with my uncle, and I learned so much from him. I assure you, whatever my uncle says is the absolute truth and nothing less.

The following week passed uneventfully, and we enjoyed our time in the laboratory together. The days that weren't filled with too many experiments, he had the opportunity to show me many basic laws of science. This included the basic laws of physics which states bodies at rest tend to stay at rest and bodies in motion tend to stay in motion. Most days we ate lunch together, and I enjoyed that time so very much. There were days in which he would give me a tour of some of the areas of the college that weren't off-limits. I actually found that interesting in the sense of higher learning. In the future, when I write my autobiography, my readers will learn that I only went to the ninth grade. Higher learning was not my cup of tea. I don't want to sound like I'm bragging, but I am self-taught. I've given thousands of speeches around the world, and my audiences have thought that I have two or three PhDs. I'm always thrilled to be complimented like that, but it's not the truth.

Before I knew it, the following weekend was here, and I was very excited for the simple reason that our visit to the secret place by the pond was approaching. Our next installment, for lack of a better word, was coming, and I couldn't wait.

"Stevie, this time when we leave for our place by the pond, let's pack a big lunch so we can eat and watch the ducks and their babies when we are done talking."

"Uncle, with all of your brains, why haven't you ever suggested that before?"

"Well, Stevie, with all of your abilities and your sharpness of mind, why haven't you suggested that? For God's sake, do I have to think for both of us?"

"Well, Uncle, come to think of it, that's a great idea, why don't you?"

"Okay, okay, little one, don't be a wiseass like your father. I've had a stomach full of his mind growing up. How about we make ourselves that big picnic lunch and head out to our place by the pond."

"That sounds great to me, Uncle, let's do it."

When we arrived at our special place, the sun was shining so brightly, and the temperature was in the seventies with hardly any humidity.

"Okay, Stevie, I'm going to talk to you about watchers. Our planet has been watched for a very long time. The people around the globe that come from different walks of life and are very respected in their own right say they have seen what has been called UFOs.

"You can believe it. They have really seen these objects. They are not all the same looking. Their ships come in different shapes and sizes. There are some that are oval, round, and then there are the bigger ships, I have learned, that are wedge shaped, like a piece of apple pie. Those are ships that have the aliens that look similar to us. The so-called little gray people are the workers that take orders from the aliens that are like us. And by the way I assure you, there are no such beings as little green men.

"We have been watched for thousands of years, I am told. You may ask, why haven't they landed and, for lack of a better phrase, introduced themselves? They aren't ready. They are not our enemies. The aliens believe, because we are still a warring planet, we would misuse their technology, and I'm afraid they're right. I agree that our generals would take their advanced weapons and control the earth in a way that is not right. Their desire is to help further our growth, not to cause a war that could and would destroy the earth.

"The aliens have antigravitational technology, lasers that are much bigger and much more powerful than our little dingy ones in our laboratories. Also, on their planets they have a system by which any asteroids or large meteors can be destroyed with the push of a button. And get a load of this, Stevie, they have this astonishing ability to shield their planet against any other warring planet or planets that may decide to hit them with powerful missiles that would otherwise destroy their planet. They have no diseases such as cancer or arthritis, and their average life span is 150 years old. So as you can readily see, for those and other reasons, they are not ready to share their knowledge with us."

"Uncle, what you have told me is incredible, and I believe what you have said to me, but it's a lot to take in."

"Yes, it is, but it's quite true. I have seen with my own eyes examples of what they can do, and believe you me, they can do exactly as they have stated.

"Maybe, just maybe in the future if we ever can prove that we can be trusted as a race of people, we would be part of an organization of planets that run the unknown part of the universe. Furthermore, they would share the secrets of galactic space travel, traveling to other planets and galaxies in almost a blink of your eye. So, little one, is that enough for today? I hope so, Stevie, because I am starving. Let's eat, okay."

"Okay, Uncle, I agree that's plenty of information for one day. Let's eat."

The next week past very quickly. There were a lot of meetings my uncle had to attend that I was not privy to. There was one experiment that I was in attendance for. The expectation for this particular experiment was to change the molecular makeup of this object. The object in question was a glass, a plain glass without any liquid in it. By bombarding this glass with certain waves, they were able to change its design. It worked. When the glass was examined, it now resembled a bucket. The proof of the pudding is in the eating. The experiment worked. The application for this experiment proved that molecular makeup can be changed. Being that we are made up of molecules, it is possible in the future to change our molecules and transport us from one place to another while rearranging our molecules back the way they were at our destination. Therefore, teleportation, as it is called, is possible in the future.

Before I knew it, Friday evening was upon us. We had a great dinner and relaxed, playing Monopoly. I lost again, as usual. Maybe with enough patience, I can beat my uncle someday at this money game.

It was supposed to rain on Sunday, so we decided to go to the park the next day on Saturday. It was a very hot day, you know, the three Hs—hot, hazy, and humid. The discussion for today was very general, so we sat by the ducks and their babies.

"Now, let me tell you, Stevie, there is one particular subject that really pisses me off, and that is the description of the little aliens that are the workers. They are not little green men, they are gray in color. One would have to be color blind not to see gray. Personally, I have no idea where people game up with the color green. I have been in the same room with them for many hours, and I assure you they are gray. They take their orders directly from the human-looking aliens.

"There is a story I want to share with you of the greatest importance. We need to go to our secret place for me to tell you this adventure. So let's take a little walk to the other side of the pond."

We had a nice casual walk to the other side of the pond, where we have shared the most guarded information in human history.

Without any notice, I was plucked from my living room one night at about seven o'clock. When I asked these darkly dressed men where they were taking me, all they would say is, 'Sit back and relax, Professor. You will know soon enough where you're going. Please sit there and enjoy the trip.'

I was taken to what appeared to be a private air-strip where I was joined with a group of men and women numbering somewhere around twenty.

We were told to enter this rather large craft that didn't look at all familiar.

First of all, it was nothing that I had ever seen before. The inside was not familiar to me in anyway. Secondly, when we took off it wasn't taxiing down the airstrip. It took off vertically. Thirdly, there was no sound of any engines that I could heard.

I'll tell you this, as we climbed up, up, and away, I looked around at the group, and I noticed right off the strangest looks that I had ever seen on people. Then, all of a sudden we shot forward like a stone in a slingshot. It pushed us back in our seats and kept us there for what seemed to be an eternity.

Then, as before, without any notice we made an abrupt stop. We started dropping in altitude and finally felt Mother Earth. We were told to exit the aircraft, and when we did, we all were met with an ice-cold wind. It appeared we were in the center with high snowbanks around us.

We were then herded into this large carrier with tracks like a bulldozer would have. Within a few minutes, we were at our destination. From the carrier, we were taken into the largest elevator I have ever seen in my entire life. It was dimly lit, but it was big enough to fit all twenty of us plus two armed guards and a strange-looking little gray man that looked like ET.

This large elevator started to drop fast, very fast. We must have dropped thirty or forty seconds worth before we came to a stop.

The elevator opened into what looked like a gymnasium you might see in any high school. As we approached the middle of this large expanse, I could see in the middle were a few rows of chairs, with a long table in front. Sitting at this table, where some of the strangest figures I had ever seen in my life. We all sat down in any of the three rows of chairs, and we waited. Out came a man dressed in armed forces clothes with a lot of ribbons and medals on his chest. He introduced himself as General Hanson, head of the Armed Forces Committee.

"Ladies and gentlemen, I know it's very late and you have had quite a mysterious trip. You will all know the answers you are no doubt looking for very shortly.

"Before we begin, let me express my deepest appreciation to all of you that are here. All of you are witnessing what most human beings will never see. It is the dawn of a new age, an age of discovery and knowledge beyond your wildest dreams.

"Let me introduce our most distinguished guests in front of you. First from left to right, that is Commander Nelson, head of our worldwide navy fleet. Next to him, General Robertson, in charge of our army worldwide. Next is Robert Masterson, FBI director for the good old USA. Next is Timothy Carlson, director of the CIA, and last but not least is the Supreme Commander of the Organization of Planetary Affairs. Because no one is able to pronounce his real name, just refer to him as Supreme Commander.

"The Supreme Commander comes from a system far beyond our Milky Way galaxy. He has traveled literally millions and millions of miles to join us today at this most glorious occasion."

If you could see my uncle's face as well as the others', you would see expressions frozen in one position and hanging on every word being said by General Hanson.

"Now, ladies and gentlemen, let me introduce the Supreme Commander of the Organization of Planets. Please save any questions until he is through talking to all of you. Supreme Commander, the floor is yours."

"People of the planet Earth, let me first say, we come in peace. You are wondering how I speak your language. We have been watching and listening to your planet for thousands of years, not me personally, but our race."

At that moment, my uncle told me, everyone laughed. They knew the Supreme Commander wasn't thousands of years old, but it was funny nevertheless.

"Our race's average life span is 150 years old. We have no violence on our planets. Those that still choose to be warring planets are not a member of our culture, nor are they members of our organization of planets. We have learned to go above and beyond criminal behavior.

"Our mission was to wait and watch and listen to the planet Earth. We have much to offer you such as curing your diseases, all of them and advancing your technology many hundreds of years. But you as a race of earthlings have never been ready to our satisfaction. That is why we have never made ourselves known to you as far as landing our ships and addressing your government, which I believe is called the United Nations Assembly.

"My race is thousands of years old, and we have been interested in you for that long. In fact, we have watched your people of the caves and studied your development forward from that time. Even from the earliest days of watching you, there has been fighting of the cave people, which has escalated into wars for the most ridiculous reasons. However, the leaders of my planet have sent me as their emissary to visit Earth in hopes that all your wars will stop. To accomplish this huge undertaking, it required me to become visible to the people on Earth.

At this point in my uncle's story to me, he mentioned that there were many questions asked that night. So many, he thought the Supreme Commander would have to stop the questions, but he didn't. Uncle told me, by the time they finished, it was three o'clock the next morning.

We were all returned to the alien ship with the warning never to repeat what had happened to anyone that night, ever. Not that anyone would believe them, but they were all warned. If anyone betrayed that warning, there would be stiff consequences. Frankly, no one at that meeting in Alaska wanted to know what those stiff consequences would be.

Once everyone was home, the group went back to their own routines. However, my uncle assured me that those people that were present at that secret meeting in Alaska were never quite the same again, and I certainly believe him. The obvious reason is that my uncle was never quite the same again. He tells me his ideas and way of life became different. His thoughts and actions had somewhat changed—for the better. As far as my uncle was concerned, he assured me that he had never uttered a word about that night until now, and that was because he trusted me completely. I will always love him for that and much more for the rest of my life.

The summer was passing rapidly. It was the middle of August with only a month left to visit with my uncle. You know that old saying, "Time flies when you're having fun"?

It was the fifth year of discovery, and I had discovered so much. At that time in my life, the one wish I had for myself was that I would remember all that I had learned from my uncle these past five years. With one month left to go, I sincerely hoped there would be much more to learn. I was about to find out; wishes do come to fruition.

"Stevie, another weekend is at hand, and I have been thinking about doing something different with part of it."

"What did you have in mind, Uncle?"

"Well, Stevie, I would like you to think of something special I can get you. I would like to take you shopping for something you would like, something you could take back home from me to you."

"Uncle, that's very nice of you, but you don't have to do anything. You have given me more than enough in the way of special things."

"Stevie, I know I don't have to, but I want to! So you be thinking of that one thing you would like to take home from me to you, okay? Will you do that for an old man?"

"Uncle, in my mind you're not old, you're my uncle, you will live on forever in my mind."

"That's very beautiful of you, Stevie, thank you. Let's get showered and dressed so we can get out of this house and have some fun."

So shopping we went, and fun we had. My uncle even bought lunch while we were out. We had a great time together. Oh! I almost forgot to tell you what he bought me. He bought me a t-shirt with his picture on it and underneath it said, "For every action, there is an opposite and equal reaction." This is one of the many laws of physics. Little did I know what the near future would have in store for the uncle I loved so. How very little we really know about what is to come tomorrow and the next day after that. I'm truthful enough to admit, when you think you know something, you find out you don't really know it at all.

The next morning started out with a beautiful sunrise. As the sun rose, it took that sadness away from my heart even though I knew I would be leaving in two weeks.

It was Sunday, of course, and we were going to our secret place at the pond. Somehow I got the distinct impression that it was going to be a winning day, and believe me I wasn't disappointed.

After witnessing that sunrise, I hopped out of bed and got cleaned up and dressed in record time. As usual, my uncle had it timed to the minute. Breakfast had just been put on the table as I walked into the kitchen.

"Good morning, Uncle, I'm starved."

"You always are, Stevie, you have the appetite of two. Sit down while I get you a cold glass of milk."

After a most successful breakfast, as usual, we rinsed and stacked the dishes, then off we went to the secret place at the pond.

"Stevie, the most guarded secret in recorded history was the Manhattan Project. It had to do with ending World War II. I was responsible for splitting the atom and, in doing so, the creation of fusion. Simply put, the bombarding of neutrons and electrons in relation to the radioactive material housed in the bomb caused a chain reaction which produced the atomic bomb. The idea behind the testing was to drop two bombs, one on Hiroshima and one at Nagasaki. It surely ended the war, but at a great death toll. The collateral damage was immense. What I mean by collateral damage is innocent men, women, and children. The bombs were set to go off somewhere around ten thousand feet, and by doing so, around one hundred thousand human beings were disintegrated immediately, and millions died of radiation poisoning over a relatively short time.

"Personally speaking, it was a double-edged sword for me. On one side, it was enough to stop the Imperial Japanese forces from killing our men and women and end the war. But on the other side of the sword, there were so many innocent people who had to die as a result of the bomb. Since 1945, I have felt very guilty at what I had created even though it ended the war.

"Then, if that wasn't difficult enough, during the bomb's infancy, which was testing and the actual building of the two bombs, I had to put up with another scientist, who was also a professor of physics, his name was Robert Oppenheimer.

"In the first place, he made people think that he was the head of the Manhattan Project even though he damn well knew that I was. In the second place, he was always in front of the cameras and on television. That was before the Manhattan Project and after the news was released. Robert Oppenheimer was a very narcissistic human being. What that really means, little one, is he was full of himself, self-love but in a very vain way. Most people couldn't stand to be in the same room with him more than a few minutes. Of course, you must realize also that he was very jealous of me. Why? I'll never know. For God's sake, he was very famous in his own right. It must have been because I was short or something, ha ha ha. Actually, Robert Oppenheimer was in fact very tall compared to me.

"Stevie, I am not trying to complain about anything. I did what I had to do under very stressful times on this planet. Even though it is 1955, I predict we are not done with wars, not by a long shot. Human beings start wars for the most ridiculous reasons.

"It might be for greed or power or even religion. But I do predict that man will kill man, not missiles.

"Stevie, I am done for today. Let's go home and pig out on some very tasty roast beef I have been saving for just this occasion. You know that it makes some mighty fine sandwiches. Let's get out of here and go home, it's been a day. Stevie, how about some checkers tonight, think you might finally beat me?"

"No, Uncle, but it will be fun trying!"

The next couple of weeks passed uneventfully. Actually, what Uncle did is take some time off from work. He had accrued vacation time that he hadn't used, so he decided to use it for me.

It was the last weekend, and Monday I would be going home, but today was only Saturday. He told me over breakfast that he wanted one more trip to the pond, preferably our secret place by the pond, for one more talk. But he wanted to use Saturday as the last secret day, because it meant that much to him, so, of course it was just fine with me.

So as we did once before, Uncle suggested we bring a big picnic lunch. We showered after breakfast and dressed casually because it was going to be very hot.

We put together cold fried chicken, potato salad he had made the night before, and some bottles of delicious springwater. About 10:00 a.m., we were off and running. We were definitely off, but not running; you know what I mean. Instead of walking to the pond, we decided to ride the bicycles that day, and it was a nice change.

Once we arrived at our secret place we got everything arranged the way we wanted it on a big blanket. Then, my uncle and I got comfortable with everything around us.

"Stevie, there is one more category I want to talk to you about. It takes place in 1947 at a place called Roswell, New Mexico.

"I don't believe it happened again, I mean being famous can be a bitch. This time it was the middle of the night, sound asleep, when I was awaken by pounding on my front door.

"Half-asleep, I went downstairs and answered the front door without looking out first to see who it was.

"Well, let me tell you, little one, I woke up pretty fast when I opened the front door. Standing in front of me were two men, and they were dressed in all black. I remember distinctly saying out loud, 'Are we going through this again? Wasn't once enough? It was for me I told them.' I was told the same thing as before. 'Professor Einstein, you are needed, please get dressed, you're coming with us.' 'Well, fellas, here we go again.'

"So I got dressed and, may I add, this time it was in record time. We ended up at a different private airstrip, and it was a private jet and certainly government issue. This time the flight, according to my watch, took four hours.

"We landed at a private airstrip in the desert just before dawn. We were all herded into a rather large installation on the ground floor, no elevators and no thousand feet underground.

"We were brought into what resembled a large hangar. On the ground, the hanger was filled with some kind of wreckage, which I didn't understand at the time, it was the wreckage of an alien aircraft we were told, that had crashed about five to seven miles outside of Roswell in the desert.

"We were given a tour of the wreckage. None of which resembled any kind of aircraft I had ever seen. The group was brought into a large conference room. We were told, in fact, it was an alien craft, and there were four aliens aboard. Three aliens died on impact, but there was one still alive, and he was in really bad shape.

"Then we were shown a piece of material, shiny in nature, but no matter which way it was folded, it returned to its flat shape. No matter what you tried to do to it, it couldn't be destroyed. It couldn't be ripped or torn with any kind of scissor. The material, as strong as it seemed, was impervious to any harm.

"If that wasn't incredible enough, we were told that we would be seeing the only survivor of the crash. Even though we would be behind a glass window for our protection, we would be able to observe this little gray being.

"After we were given specific instructions, we rode another large elevator far below the ground floor. The elevator opened into what looked exactly like a large science fair. People were walking fast from one side to the other all dressed in white. Their heads were covered in protective hoods with masks across their face.

"We were told exactly where to stand, and all of a sudden one of the scientists flicked a switch, and the large panel in front of us slid to the side. In front of us was a little gray figure on an operating table. Surrounding the gray figure were several doctors working to, no doubt, try and save its life.

"My uncle told me that you could hear everyone breathing. You could cut the quiet with a knife. You could even hear a pin drop. Then we were told the little gray alien died. The doctors did everything they could, but it wasn't enough, not nearly enough.

Without knowing alien physiology, it was almost impossible to save his life, but they still tried."

The sadness in that room was overwhelming. There were scientists crying, number one, at the loss of a life, and two, the knowledge of what happened to make them crash was lost forever. Even my uncle Albert was very saddened that night at the loss.

A short time later, our government was contacted by the alien's home world. The message was short and sweet. They wished the bodies of the crew returned. It wasn't but a few days later that the alien ship landed and removed the bodies from Roswell to bring back to their home planet for their own ceremonies. My uncle cried as the four little figures were brought out and carried onto their ship.

That next day, all twenty of the scientists were flown back home to their respective cities, and my uncle never saw them again.

"That was the story of Roswell, New Mexico, 1947. It was real, it happened, and I was present to see it. I will admit to you, Stevie, that I never want to go through something like that ever again."

Sunday night my uncle and I just relaxed and talked. Being that it was my last night at Princeton, he called out for dinner to be delivered. That was a nice treat as well as a nice surprise.

Monday morning came too fast. When my uncle woke me up to get ready for Joseph's arrival, it was pouring cats and dogs. What a miserable day to travel home.

About ten o'clock, Joseph knocked on the front door. It was great to see him, and at the same time, I would be saying good-bye to my uncle for another year.

I hadn't been home but a few days when my father called me into his office.

"Stevie, I have some very bad news to tell you. Your uncle Albert has passed away from a massive coronary. I know how much you love him, and he loved you. Why don't you take the rest of the day off and just do whatever you want to. I am truly sorry for your loss. Believe it or not, I really thought he was a good man who only did good things to help this planet and the people on it. I know he will be missed by a lot of people."

I walked out of my father's office absolutely devastated. I didn't want to talk to anyone the rest of the day, and I didn't. I will miss my uncle Albert more than I can possibly put into words. With much regret, I am sticking to this story, and all of its content. My uncle will never be replaced in my lifetime and I never want him to be. So good bye uncle. I love you and will always think of you, and all that you have taught me. Good bye, my friend.

Aftermath: My Final Thoughts

In the future, if there is to be one, it remains to be seen what will happen to our beautiful planet and the people who inhabit it. Without people like my uncle Albert, your guess is as good as mine.

People like you and I can only hope that the ones who make the real decisions make the right ones. If they choose not to because of their obsessive thirst for power, greed, and, let's not forget, money, our planet is as good as dead, uninhabitable.

I know one thing beyond a shadow of a doubt, being the last Einstein on Earth—it won't take long to ruin the rest of our home. The key phrase in this message is "Our planet." It's everyone's home, and if we don't take care of it, it won't take care of us.

Personally speaking, I only have one question, Is there another Albert Einstein in the house?

Do you know the answer?

I sincerely hope you have enjoyed these memoirs as much as I have enjoyed writing them.

I hope you'll look for my first novel, entitled *Nightwalker*. Let me assure you it's not about vampires or prostitutes. It's not even about the walking dead. Haven't we had enough of that?

Nightwalker is about good against evil. The book is a page-turner and fast-paced. The characters are fixed in place and ready for your enjoyment.

Mathew Connor is the star of show, and fighting for world domination is the very cold-blooded and evil Arthur Benning.

The FBI call their hero just Connor. He is the best of the best. He is a loyal husband and great father. Read how Arthur Benning tries to destroy Connor's world from *A* to *Z* all for the domination of the world. Arthur will stop at nothing to possess the blue star and win the game, planet Earth. To accomplish his mission, Arthur must have Connor's help. Once Arthur has the blue star, he will be able to run the earth. Then and only then will he make sure that Connor and his family are never heard from again in this world.

About the Author

By the time I was born, my two sisters, Greta and Doris, where much older. I was the baby and the very last male Einstein to be born.

On that September 10th day in 1945 when I came into this world, breach birth, my father Alfred Einstein had already owned twenty-seven companies. He was, in fact, a bonafide billionaire. In addition to owning that many companies, he was laundering money for the Sicilian Mafia since he was twenty-one. Unfortunately he didn't listen to anyone about his smoking of five packs of Camels per day because he died of cancer at age 59.

Because of Mom and Dad's extreme wealth, I hardly ever saw them. If it wasn't for my nanny, Josephine and my bodyguard Joseph, all I would be seeing everyday would be four walls and my toys.

Like many other people, I had to grow up fast. Before I knew it, I enlisted in the Navy after my schooling, rather than be drafted. Young in life, I believed in the American flag, and the freedom it afforded everyone and the chance for children to be children before they have to face the full brunt of life.

After the Navy, I joined the Peace Corps with a great opportunity to help people for two years in the Middle East. The most valuable lesson I had learned working with people on the other side of the word is, all of us have the same emotions. The only real difference is food and dress.

After the Peace Corps, I was fortunate to work in the state and federal government. I enjoyed my work immensely. Isn't that half the battle? After many years of rewarding work, I retired.

Shortly after retiring, I received the worst news I had ever gotten, my oldest sister who I loved more than my own life was dying of a brain tumor. Without any reservation, I'll tell you Greta was the most courageous person I've ever known to date. Before she died, she had a vision of me in a dream. She told me I would be a very successful writer. She said it was my creativity that was uncanny. A few years after she passed away, I was accepted in the largest writing school in this country. I learned so much about writing and myself over those two years. After just a short time of entering the school, my teacher Lois told me that I had the so called "X factor" they all look for as teachers. I honor Lois with this first book and want to prove her right.

Consequently, seven years later, here we are, you and I with "My Uncle Albert" my first book which happens to chronicle my time spent with my uncle. After its release in the very near future, will come my first novel, "*Nightwalker.*" After that, five sequels are planned, the first one being, "*Midnight Man,*" which I have started.

With Page Publishing and many excited readers, I will feel a great sense of accomplishment for myself and my readers. My deepest desires are to bring my readers around the world to different times, different places, and to take them away from the everyday problems we all have.

So, I will always remain you're loyal author,

Stephen I. Einstein

CPSIA information can be obtained at www.ICGtesting.com
Printed in the USA
BVOW07s0419050215

386402BV00001B/9/P